INTRODUCTION

To the Teacher

The ability to sight-read fluently is now more than ever an essential skill ⟨…⟩ professional and amateur. Yet the *study* of sight-reading is often badly neglected by y⟨…⟩⟨…⟩s, and is frequently regarded as no more than an unpleasant side-line in their training. The purpose of this workbook is to incorporate sight-reading into regular practice and lessons, and to help prepare young students for the sight-reading tests in grade examinations. It is intended as a source of motivation, offering a progressive series of enjoyable and stimulating stages in which the student will have the opportunity to show considerable improvement from week to week.

The sight-reading exercises and questions are related to the requirements of grades five to eight. An approximate guide to standard is as follows:

Stages 1 to 3	= Grade 5
Stages 4 to 6	= Grade 6
Stages 6 to 9	= Grade 7
Stages 9 to 12	= Grade 8

Each stage consists of two parts: firstly, two pages of work to be prepared by the student in advance, consisting of preliminary rhythmic and melodic exercises, and then a short piece with related questions; and secondly, an unprepared test. (These tests – three examples for each stage – are to be found at the end of the book.)

The student's work can be assessed using the marking scheme outlined below.

Marking

Each stage carries a maximum of 50 marks:

15 marks maximum for the rhythmic and melodic exercises
15 marks for the combined questions and prepared test
20 marks for the unprepared test (You should devise a similar series of questions for the unprepared test, and take the student's answers into account when allocating a final mark.)

Space is given at the end of each stage to maintain a running total so that progress may be clearly observed.

To the Student

The ability to sight-read fluently is a most important part of your training as a player, whether you intend to play professionally, or simply for enjoyment. If you become a good sight-reader you will be able to learn pieces more quickly and to play in ensembles and orchestras with confidence. Furthermore, in grade examinations, good performance in the sight-reading test will result in useful extra marks.

How to use the workbook

The book is divided into 12 stages. Each stage introduces one or more new features, which appear at the top of the left-hand page. As you begin to reach higher levels your aim in sight-reading should now not only be to play notes and rhythms accurately, but also to observe all markings of expression and to give character to your performance. You should prepare the exercises in each stage carefully and your teacher will mark your work according to accuracy. There are normally four different types of exercise in each stage:

1 **Rhythmic exercises.** It is very important that you should be able to feel and maintain a steady beat. The purpose of the *rhythmic exercises* will help you develop this ability. There are at least four ways of using these exercises. You should try them all:

1 Clap or tap the lower line (the beat) while singing the upper line to 'la'.

2 Tap the lower line with your foot and clap the upper line.

3 On a table or flat surface, tap the lower line with one hand and the upper line with the other. Also try this method reversing the parts giving each hand an attempt at the upper line.

4 'Play' the lower line on a metronome and clap or tap the upper line. Try this at varying speeds.

Always clap or tap two bars before you begin the upper line, in order to establish the beat.

2 **Melodic exercises.** Fluent sight-reading depends on recognising melodic shapes at first glance. These shapes are generally related to scales and arpeggios. Thorough knowledge of scales and arpeggios is therefore invaluable in developing fluent sight-reading. Always notice the *key-signature*, and the notes affected by it; and any *accidentals* before you begin.

3 **A prepared piece with questions.** On the next page you will find a short *piece*, which you should also prepare carefully, together with a set of *questions*. The questions are similar to those asked at some grade examinations, and are there to help you think about and understand the piece before you play it. Put your answers in the spaces provided.

4 **An unprepared piece.** Finally, your teacher will give you an *unprepared* test to be read *at sight*. Make sure you look at the *time-signature*, the *key-signature*, *accidentals* and the *dynamic levels*.

Remember to count throughout each piece and to keep going at a steady and even tempo. Always try to look ahead and *imagine* the pitch of the next note.

You will be awarded marks out of a total of 50 for each stage. There is a box provided at the end of each stage so that you can keep a running total of your marks as you progress.

Transposition

The act of transposition means seeing one note and playing another at some particular interval above or below it. Many of the exercises and pieces both in this book and in *Improve Your Sight-reading Grades I-V* can be used for transposition practice.

Orchestral trumpet and horn players have to transpose much of the time. The transpositions most often met in orchestral parts are those for the A, C, D, E flat, E and F instruments. The transpositions listed below are for use with the B flat instrument. The following comments should be noted:

A transposition:	play every note as a flat.
C transposition:	play up one tone
D transposition:	play up a major 3rd
E♭ transposition:	play up a perfect 4th
E transposition:	play up an augmented 4th
F transposition:	play up a perfect 5th

Like the transposition for A, the E transposition can be read as for trumpet in F, but again flattening every note. The best way to become efficient in transposing is to PRACTISE REGULARLY.

The accomplished sight-reader

To become a truly accomplished sight-reader it is necessary to play both accurately *and* musically. In addition to pitch and rhythmic accuracy, this also involves observing notational signs and symbols and expression markings. Below are most of the standard signs with some guidance for their interpretation. A knowledge of the standard Italian terms is essential.

The staccatissimo

The wedge indicates that a note should have a strong stress and be considerably shortened.

The staccato

Notes marked with a dot should be played lightly and without accent. They should be played for about half their written value though this will depend partly on the style of the music.

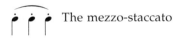 The mezzo-staccato

Mezzo-staccato notes should be gently separated without interrupting the flow of the music.

This symbol indicates a gentle emphasis and very slight shortening of the note.

Marking the final note in a phrase with a dot indicates an abrupt ending. Play the final note for about half its written value.

The tenuto mark or agogic accent

Notes marked with this symbol should have a slight but maintained stress, and should be held for their full written value.

> or ∧

These marks indicate that a note should begin with a degree of intensity greater than the marked dynamic level. ∧, which is less common than >, indicates a heavier accent.

sf, sff, rf, sfz

These symbols indicate a sudden and forceful surging in volume. The degree of loudness much depends on the dynamic level of other notes in the passage.

fp

This symbol indicates a short, but distinct *forte* which changes quickly to *piano*. The change to *piano* may be made abruptly or as a rapid *diminuendo*, depending on context.

4

STAGE 1

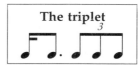

RHYTHMIC EXERCISES

MELODIC EXERCISES

Mark: [ ]

PREPARED PIECE

1 What does *Allegro ma non troppo* indicate?

2 In which key is this piece?

3 Clap the rhythm:

In which bar does it occur?

4 Put a cross above the B flats.

5 What does the symbol indicate?

6 Which bar is based on the arpeggio of C major?

Total:

Allegro ma non troppo

Mark:

Prepared work total:

Unprepared:

Total:

STAGE 2

More rhythms in $\frac{3}{8}$ and $\frac{5}{8}$

RHYTHMIC EXERCISES

MELODIC EXERCISES

Mark:

PREPARED PIECE

1   What does *Allegretto* indicate?

2   What will you count?

3   In which key is the piece written?

4   Bar 9 represents an arpeggio of C minor; what arpeggios form bar 10?

5   Mark the A flat with a cross.

6   What does *mp* indicate?

Total:

Allegretto

Mark:

Prepared work total:

Unprepared:

Total:

Running totals:

1   2

STAGE 3

RHYTHMIC EXERCISES

MELODIC EXERCISES

Mark:

PREPARED PIECE

1 What does *Andante con moto* indicate?

2 In which key is the piece written?

3 What will you count?

4 In which bar do the notes of an arpeggio of B flat major occur?

5 What does *rall.* indicate?

6 Where does the rhythm in bar 3 re-appear?

Total:

Andante con moto

Mark:

Prepared work total:

Unprepared:

Total:

Running totals:

1	2	3

STAGE 4

RHYTHMIC EXERCISES

MELODIC EXERCISES

Mark:

PREPARED PIECE

1 What does *Allegro giocoso* indicate?

2 In which key is the piece?

3 How are the notes marked ♩ to be played?

4 What does the sign > indicate?

5 What does *cresc.* indicate?

6 Clap the rhythm: **3/4** 𝅘𝅥 𝅘𝅥 𝅘𝅥 𝅘𝅥 𝅘𝅥 | 𝅗𝅥 ——— (bar 4)

Total:

Allegro giocoso

Mark:

Prepared work total:

Unprepared:

Total:

Running totals:

1	2	3	4

STAGE 5

A and E flat major; C minor

MELODIC EXERCISES

Mark:

PREPARED PIECE

1   What does *Allegretto con moto* indicate?

2   In which key is the piece?

3   What will you count?

4   How are the notes marked ♩ to be played?

5   In which bar does an arpeggio of G major occur?

6   Mark the first A flat with a cross.

Total:

Allegretto con moto

Mark:

Prepared work total:

Unprepared:

Total:

Running totals:

1	2	3	4	5

STAGE 6

 7 and 7 rests

RHYTHMIC EXERCISES

1

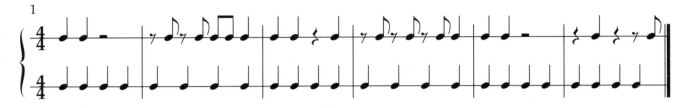

2

3

MELODIC EXERCISES

Mark:

PREPARED PIECE

1 What does *Andante con moto* indicate?

2 In which key is the piece written?

3 What does the marking ♩ indicate?

4 What will you count?

5 Where is the rhythm in bar 1 repeated?

6 What is the character of the piece?

Total:

Andante con moto

Mark:

Prepared work total:

Unprepared:

Total:

Running totals:

1	2	3	4	5	6

STAGE 7

RHYTHMIC EXERCISES

When crotchet and quaver metres are juxtaposed, always ensure that you 'feel' the quaver subdivision throughout the exercise. The small notes (showing the subdivisions) are to help you.

MELODIC EXERCISES

Mark:

PREPARED PIECE

1 What does *Con brio* mean?

2 How will you count this piece?

3 How are the notes marked ♩ to be played?

4 Which bar demands the softest dynamic level?

5 What does *senza rit.* mean?

6 How are the notes marked ♩ to be played?

Total:

Prepared work total:

Unprepared:

Total:

Running totals:

1	2	3	4	5	6	7

STAGE 8

MELODIC EXERCISES

1

2

3

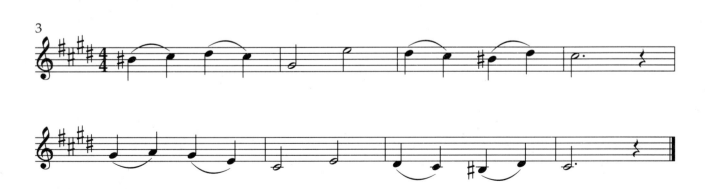

Mark:

PREPARED PIECE

1   What does *Allegro con moto* mean?   ☐

2   In which key is the piece written?   ☐

3   What does the time signature ¢ indicate?   ☐

4   What does *leggiero* mean?   ☐

5   What do the markings ♩ indicate?   ☐

6   What do *cresc.* and *rall.* mean?   ☐

                                              Total: ☐

                                              Mark: ☐

Prepared work total: ☐

Unprepared: ☐

Total: ☐

Running totals:

1	2	3	4	5	6	7	8

STAGE 9

$\dfrac{7}{8}$

RHYTHMIC EXERCISES

MELODIC EXERCISES

1

2

3

Mark:

PREPARED PIECE

1 What does *Con grazia* mean?

2 In which key is the piece written?

3 What do the markings ♩ indicate?

4 What will you count?

5 What does *cantabile* mean?

6 Add, under an appropriate two-bar phrase, the dynamic shape: ◁ ▷

Total:

Con grazia

Mark:

Prepared work total:

Unprepared:

Total:

Running totals:

1	2	3	4	5	6	7	8	9

STAGE 10

$\frac{9}{8}$ and $\frac{12}{8}$

RHYTHMIC EXERCISES

By this stage you should be able *instinctively* to decide in which of two ways to count compound time.
If the pulse is slow, it is usually safer to count quavers. If the pulse is fast, then it may be easier to count in beats (i.e. dotted crotchets in 6/8, 9/8, or 12/8) but ensure that you are still able to 'feel' the subdivisions.

Practise the following using both methods:

MELODIC EXERCISES

Mark:

PREPARED PIECE

1 What does *Dolce* indicate?

2 What will you count?

3 In which key is the piece?

4 Which bars contain the tonic arpeggio?

5 How will you achieve the character of the piece?

6 What does *calando* indicate?

Total:

Mark:

Prepared work total:

Unprepared:

Total:

Running totals:

1	2	3	4	5	6	7	8	9	10

STAGE 11

Other forms of triplets in simple time

RHYTHMIC EXERCISES

MELODIC EXERCISES

Mark:

PREPARED PIECE

1 What does *Lento espressivo* mean?

2 In which key is the piece written?

3 What will you count?

4 What does *molto rall.* indicate?

5 What does the sign over the final note indicate?

6 Which is the loudest bar in the piece?

Total:

Mark:

Prepared work total:

Unprepared:

Total:

Running totals:

1	2	3	4	5	6	7	8	9	10	11

STAGE 12

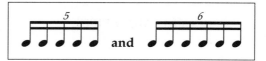

RHYTHMIC EXERCISES

MELODIC EXERCISES

Mark: ☐

PREPARED PIECE

1 What does *Andante* mean?

2 In what key is the piece written?

3 What will you count?

4 What is the character of the music and how will you achieve it?

5 How will you interpret the marking ♩ ♩ ?

6 What does *sonore* indicate?

Total:

Mark:

Prepared work total:

Unprepared:

Total:

Running totals:

1	2	3	4	5	6	7	8	9	10	11	12

CONCLUSION

A sight-reading checklist

Before you begin to play a piece at sight, always remember to consider the following:

1   Look at the key-signature.

2   Look at the time-signature.

3   Find the notes which need raising or lowering.

4   Take note of any accidentals.

5   Notice scale and arpeggio patterns.

6   Work out leger-line notes if necessary.

7   Notice dynamic and other markings.

8   Count one bar before you begin, to establish the speed.

When performing your sight-reading piece, always remember to:

1   Count yourself in with at least one bar in your chosen tempo and
    CONTINUE TO COUNT THROUGHOUT THE PIECE.

2   Keep going at a steady and even tempo.

3   Ignore mistakes.

4   Look ahead – at least to the next note.

5   Play *musically*.

UNPREPARED TESTS
STAGE 1

1 Andante

2 Scherzando

3 Alla marcia

STAGE 2

1   Moderato grazioso

2   Allegretto con moto

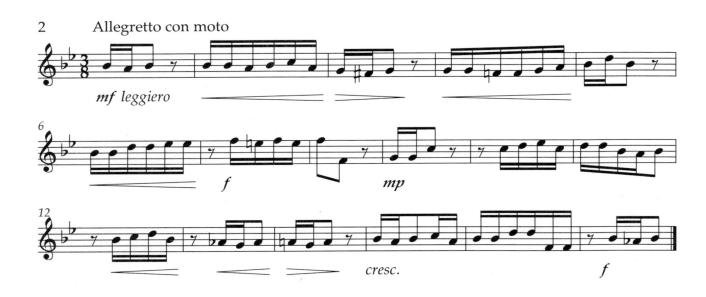

3   Poco allegretto

STAGE 3

STAGE 4

1   Allegro con brio

2   Allegretto

3   Vivace

STAGE 5

1   Andante sostenuto

2   Allegro animato

3   Allegro con brio

STAGE 6

1 Adagio ma non troppo

STAGE 7

STAGE 8

1 Presto assai

2 Lento misterioso

3 Vigoroso

STAGE 9

1   Allegretto

2   Allegro moderato

3   Allegro con fuoco

STAGE 10

STAGE 11

1 Giocoso

2 Allegro animato

3 Allegro con fuoco

STAGE 12